This book is published strictly for historical purposes.
The Naval and Military Press Ltd
expressly bears no responsibility or liability of any type,
to any first, second or third party, for any harm,
injury or loss whatsoever.

ERNEST GRUHN,
(Amateur Champion Wrestler of England.)

Published by

The Naval & Military Press Ltd
Unit 5 Riverside, Brambleside
Bellbrook Industrial Estate
Uckfield, East Sussex
TN22 1QQ England

Tel: +44 (0)1825 749494

www.naval-military-press.com
www.nmarchive.com

In reprinting in facsimile from the original, any imperfections are inevitably reproduced and the quality may fall short of modern type and cartographic standards.

THE TEXT-BOOK OF WRESTLING

BY

ERNEST GRUHN

Amateur Champion Wrestler of England

The Naval & Military Press Ltd

ILLUSTRATIONS

FIG.		PAGE
1.	"Taking Hold"	17
2.	"Block" to Waist Grip	18
3.	Head and Crotch Throw	19
4.	Chancery and Swing Over	21
5.	Waist Hold	22
6.	Arm Hold and Back Heel	24
7.	Another Arm Throw and Counter	25
8.	Half-Nelson Parry and Throw to Arm Hold	27
9.	A Standing Half-Nelson	28
10.	Side Arm Lever Hold	30
11.	A Block to the Leg Grip	31
12.	The Crotch Hold	32
13.	Waist Hold Counter to Knee Grab	34
14.	A Knee Grip Counter to Waist Hold	35
15.	The "Halch" or Head Throw	36
16.	The Double Bridge	38
17.	The Cradle Hold	39
18.	The Buttock	40
19.	Counter to Buttock and Parry	42
20.	A Standing Throw following a Safety Dive to the Mat	44
21.	A Further Waist and Crotch Hold	45
22.	The Leg Half-Nelson	46
23.	Offside, or Further Half-Nelson	48
24.	Counter and Re-Counter to Further Half-Nelson	49
25.	Counter to Half-Nelson	50
26.	Crotch Hold in Combination with Half-Nelson	52
27.	Half-Nelson and Foot Hold	53
28.	Half-Nelson Counter to Ground Leg Hold	55
29.	Ground, Head and Further Shoulder Hold	56
30.	Half-Nelson and Leg Hold	57
31.	An Unusual Fall—Counter to Ground Chancery Hold	59
32.	An Escape from a Further Shoulder Grip	60
33.	Ankle Hold Counter to Double Leg Hold	62
34.	Counter and Re-Counter to Neck and Leg Chancery Holds	63
35.	First Stage of My Favourite Ground Throw	65
36.	Second Stage	66
37.	Relwyskow's "Patent" Counter to Double Leg Ground Hold	68
38.	A Ju-jutsu Throw. Making my Opponent Throw Himself	70
39.	Waist and Neck Ground Hold	71
40.	An Under Grip—Further Shoulder and Leg Hold	73
41.	Ground Head Chancery	74
42.	Counter to Standing Chancery Hold	75

PREFACE

By the Editor of "Health and Strength"

It is certainly a reproach to the inhabitants of these islands that in order to discover a wrestler, capable of extending George Hackenschmidt, the promoters of a certain tournament should have been compelled to seek for competitors among the ranks of Continental exponents of the science.

Certain it is that they would never have been reduced to this extremity had Ernest Grühn been able to number any really promising heavy-weight wrestlers among his pupils. But the British heavy-weight is as difficult to find among the leading lights of the wrestling world as he is in the weight-lifting arena. Surely *all* our heavy-built fellow-countrymen are not too severely afflicted with sloth or indifference to put out any efforts for the honour of their country. There must be big Britons somewhere who could hold their own on the mat with the best and bulkiest foreigner if only they could find a capable instructor—an Ernie Grühn for instance, for they certainly could find no one anywhere better than he, supposing his equal to exist.

For be it understood that he has *never been thrown*

once during the last ten years, either in competition or in practice. If he were only three or four stone heavier, we should not have far to look for our World's Champion, even now that he has practically retired from serious business. He has not entered a competition for years, as he wished to let some one else have a chance to win the honours he used to carry off as regularly as clockwork. Four times Light-Weight Champion in 1898, 1900, 1901 and 1902; Middle-Weight Champion in 1900; Gold Medallist in Sandow's Wrestling Competition in 1901; winner of the 10 st. 4 lb. Competition at the Sports Exhibition at the Crystal Palace in 1904; to say nothing of hosts of open competitions at both Light and Middle Weights. Not a bad record for a man who never went 10 st. 5 lb., and could do less than that even now.

As Honorary Instructor at the German Gymnasium and at the Hammersmith Wrestling Club, he has turned out dozens of victorious wrestlers at all sorts of competitions, and at the time of writing he holds the unique record of being the Instructor and Trainer of the present champions *at all the five weights*.

He cannot, of course, give the benefits of his personal attention to *all* the promising wrestlers in the United Kingdom, but we have endeavoured to ensure that every British wrestler shall by means of this text-book enjoy at least the benefits of his written instruction, if circumstances of time and space should unfortunately debar them from the inestimable value of his personal supervision.

CHAPTER I

Points for Beginners and Hints on Training

MOST people seem to be agreed that it is impossible for any man, no matter how experienced, to teach wrestling by written instruction, and while I will admit that the feat is by no means an easy one, I do not despair of achieving the alleged impossibility in these pages, or at all events of imparting some small measure of instruction.

I do not suppose that any of my readers will imagine for one moment that they have only to study the hints and instructions contained in this little work in order to immediately qualify as champions, but I sincerely believe that I shall be able to impart certain information of value, and to put you up to certain wrinkles as to attack and defence of which you may have hitherto been in ignorance. Again, I would not wish you to imagine that I am endeavouring to assume any overweening superiority of wrestling lore, but experience has shown me that there are a vast number of men in London, as well as in the provinces, who possess many qualities which go to the making of a first-class wrestler, but who are, owing either to the lack of capable tuition or of sufficient practice, sadly ignorant of many of the most simple tricks of both attack and defence, whereby a skilled but comparatively weak man can easily establish a superiority over a far stronger but less scientific opponent.

I have therefore in these pages sought to deal more particularly with such movements, rather than with those stereotyped positions such as are commonly dealt with in wrestling text-books, since I take it that the vast majority of my readers will already be acquainted with the ordinary holds and movements. By a stroke of great good fortune I have been enabled to secure as illustrations some really excellent snapshots of an actual wrestling bout between Mr. de Relwyskow (the present Middle and Light-Weight Amateur Champion) and myself, and of another encounter between Mr. Beck (the present Heavy-Weight Champion) and Sergt. F. J. Mills, besides a few other poses and actual wrestling incidents. For these I am indebted to Messrs. Alan Cartwright & Co., who took the photographs in question, and whose reproductions will, I am sure, prove as helpful and instructive to the budding wrestler as any verbal hints of mine can possibly be.

The preliminary training of a wrestler should consist chiefly of those exercises which will best develop his muscular strength and also his all-round agility and activity.

To attain the first object, no method of training can possibly compare with heavy-weight lifting on scientific lines. Several critics have, I know, opposed practice with heavy weights, alleging that these will result in heaviness and slowness of movement.

My own experience, however, has shown me that the exact contrary is the case. All the great Continental wrestlers have developed their powers by this method, and many of them, including Hackenschmidt himself, were champion weight-lifters before they ever devoted their attention seriously to wrestling. And these men, as is well known, have demonstrated their superiority to our British heavy-weights quite as fully by their rapidity of movement as they have by their superior strength and skill.

In taking up weight-lifting as an exercise, however, it must not be supposed that any kind of method will do, for thereby the beginner will not only run the risks of overstrain and serious muscular damage, but will also probably fail to attain to anything like the same degree of strength as he would under more scientific instruction. There are so many systems of training with heavy weights that the young wrestler can easily make a selection to suit himself, but it is worthy of note that Arthur Saxon, the strongest man in the world, has accorded to Professor Inch's method the credit of being the best in existence, and that the World's Middle-Weight Weight-lifting Champion has had this claim endorsed by such practical all-round athletes as the great C. B. Fry and Tom Burrows, while several of my own pupils have adopted his system with the most satisfactory results.

All-round gymnastics, running, jumping, etc., indeed any and every form of exercise which will develop rapidity and instinctive movement, will be found most valuable ingredients of a wrestler's training. He should also practise all such free movements as will develop the muscles of his neck, such as making a bridge while supporting a weight at arm's length. He will be compelled to rely to such an extent, later on, on the resisting power of his neck and shoulders that he should *never* rest contented with the development of the muscular groups in those localities.

I do not suppose that Graeco-Roman wrestling will ever become as popular a style as the catch-as-catch-can method in this country, but I would certainly recommend all wrestlers to devote some attention to its practice.

There is no danger that Graeco-Roman practice will handicap the young wrestler in contests under the more popular code, and he will by the limitations acquire a highly desirable development in the upper part of his frame, a department in which British wrestlers, as a rule, compare unfavourably with their Continental rivals.

The would-be catch-as-catch-can champion should similarly devote a fair amount of practice to the Cumberland and Westmoreland style.

Many of his opponents will probably be very skilful ground wrestlers, but not particularly smart when on their feet. When you run up against one of these (and you can soon spot him as such by his evident anxiety to get down on the mat) refuse to follow him to earth, keep your feet, and look out for

POINTS FOR BEGINNERS 13

an early opportunity to bring off a Cumberland trip. Remember that under Amateur rules, *any two points* will give you a fall after ten minutes, and you should be able, if you are at all equally matched, to keep your own feet for that time, when almost any Cumberland and Westmoreland hold will speedily enable you to score your two points, provided of course that you are better acquainted with that form of wrestling than he is.

As already stated, I do not propose to go into any lengthy detail of the ordinary holds and throws, but a few remarks on Cumberland and Westmoreland throws, which will be found valuable in catch-as-catch-can, may be not altogether without interest here.

THE BACK HEEL,

for instance, which is the simplest of all throws; and though generally preferred by Cumberland wrestlers to the CROSS-BACK-HEEL, will not be found so valuable in the catch-hold style. The Cumberland hold renders the cross-back-heel a rather risky proceeding, but in loose-hold wrestling a very heavy fall can be brought off by its use. To back-heel your right leg goes behind his left or vice versa, you pull him in and lean your weight forward. To counter it, loose your grip, lean forward and push the other man away from you. In the cross-back-heel, your right goes behind his right and vice versa.

THE HANK OR GRAPE VINE

can be most successfully employed as a counter to the back-heel, as the other man is then leaning forward and has his attention occupied in the desire to throw *you*. As soon as you have been back-heeled, turn that side to your opponent in a flash, lift your foot, and twining your leg round his, pull him over backwards. He will generally be under the impression that it is *you* who are going, and will be frequently greatly surprised to find himself " the under dog."

In " clicking " a man, the leg is twined (either outside or inside) in similar fashion to the hank. The throws are similar to that obtained by the back-heel, save that the leg is trapped high up and the hold taken should be a tight one. A good move to get your opponent into position for a " click " is to pull him sharply forward. He will then try to steady himself by hanging back. You will then dash in with your " click," and add your weight and rush to his swing backwards.

The Outside Stroke

is a very useful trip, and should be applied by a sharp tap with your left foot against your opponent's right leg or ankle, just as you have given him a sharp pull round to the left. In tapping with the right foot you, of course, twist him to the right. It is practically the same throw as the " ankle throw " in ju-jutsu.

The Hipe or Hype

is another very useful standing throw, and can be brought into play with great success, should you have both secured a firm waist-hold. You lift your

POINTS FOR BEGINNERS

man quickly, and at the same time turn him by pressing your knee against the inside of his thigh. Lift him as high as possible before throwing him. The throw will be a better one if you make a " swinging hipe " of it, i.e. if you swing him round before applying the knee in the " hipe " itself.

All these standing throws can be brought into use at any stage of a contest, since you should always regain your feet if you judge that your antagonist is a better man at ground work than you are yourself. He may, of course, be equally superior at stand-up wrestling, but you will find, if you have practised this department thoroughly, that you are more likely to be proficient at it than he is, since the catch-hold exponent too often ignores standing throws and counters altogether.

CHAPTER II

Useful Standing Holds

THERE are several methods of

TAKING HOLD (Fig. 1)

at the commencement of a contest, but I have found the method here depicted to be the most advisable when you are opposed to a man who is at all your equal in skill and experience. You are well placed to get in a leg grip if opportunity presents itself, and are in fact equally well situated either for attack or defence, as you can keep your opponent off you fairly easily until you may wish to come to close quarters.

BLOCK TO WAIST GRIP (Fig. 2).

If you propose securing a waist grip, it is advisable to loosen suddenly from your initial hold and to press your forearm against your opponent's chin, so as to force his head back before diving for his waist, as you will thus run less risk of having your grip blocked in the manner shown in Fig. 2.

FIG. 1.
"TAKING HOLD."

Fig. 2.
"BLOCK" TO WAIST GRIP.

Fig. 3.
HEAD AND CROTCH THROW.

Head and Crotch Throw (Fig. 3).

When your waist hold is blocked by your opponent's holding you off in this manner, but with a shade less effectiveness, an opportunity arises to slip your head under his armpit, and securing a crotch-hold, to lift him off his feet, as shown in Fig. 3, when he can be thrown fairly on his back without much difficulty. This crotch and shoulder hoist may be also secured following a feint for a cross-buttock, when your opponent has stepped back a trifle to avoid that manœuvre. Even if you should not succeed in placing him square on his shoulders, you will at least bring him down heavily enough to render him incapable of long resisting your subsequently rolling him over on to them.

Chancery and Swing Over (Fig. 4).

Fig. 4 shows another method of trapping a man immediately following your initial hold.

You have secured say a head hold with your right hand on the back of your opponent's neck.

Press his head down sharply, and aiding with right shoulder pressure, force his head under your left armpit, trapping it in a chancery hold with your left arm. Slide your right arm under his left armpit and round his waist. Swing your body round to the right and push him over, pressing him down with a fair pin fall on to his shoulders. Be careful to keep his head well up with your left arm while thus pressing him over, so as to stop any attempt at making a bridge.

The Side Chancery is a variation of this hold,

FIG. 4.
CHANCERY AND SWING OVER.

Fig. 5.
WAIST HOLD.

USEFUL STANDING HOLDS

to secure which you turn in and trap him round the neck to pull him over by putting all your weight on to his neck, but is not nearly so sound, since a quick man can generally counter the move by trapping your right arm with both his and succeed in bringing off a flying mare, which will bring you to grief instead.

WAIST HOLD (Fig. 5).

Supposing you to have been successful in pushing back your opponent's head and to have avoided his attempt to block your move, you will find that a waist grip, properly applied, as shown in Fig. 5, that is to say, with your hands gripped behind his back to prevent slipping, will almost inevitably bring your man down flat on his back. Swing him round well first, hoisting him so that his feet are well clear of the ground and go over on top of him, retaining your hold.

ARM HOLD AND BACK HEEL (Fig. 6).

Another good standing throw, which you may secure while sparring for holds, is shown in Fig. 6. In this instance I managed to catch the Sergeant napping. He was feeling for a head hold, and I jumped in to the left, catching his right arm by the wrist and just above the elbow. As his right leg was advanced, I was easily able, by pressing forward and by back-heeling to cause him to overbalance, and to bring him down in a rolling fall. Provided the movement be made at the right moment, there is practically no counter to this

FIG. 6.
ARM HOLD AND BACK HEEL.

FIG. 7.
ANOTHER ARM THROW AND COUNTER.

throw, as your opponent is thrown completely off his balance and comes over easily.

ANOTHER ARM THROW AND COUNTER (Fig. 7).

Another attempted arm throw is shown in Fig. 7. Here I did not manage to catch Relwyskow off his balance, so having caught his arm as in the previous hold, turned in quickly to pull him over my right leg, but the middle and light-weight champion was too quick for me. He threw his left arm round my waist from behind, gripping his right hand, and was in a position to hoist me by a waist-hold from behind and to thus throw me down. I had to go, but by locking in with my feet as he hoisted, was able to fall on my hands and knees and to continue the struggle on the mat.

A PARRY TO THE ARM THROW (Fig. 8).

Where this arm hold has not been sufficiently secured, a good parry to the throw is to force the trapped arm free and to whip it up under the arm to the neck, securing a half-nelson. At the same time the left arm should come round the waist as before. This position is shown in Fig. 8, a hold which Beck secured on Mills, and in which the former had so freed himself as to be able to lift his opponent off his feet. Swinging him well round he threw him down, and releasing his body grip was able to press his man down with the half-nelson. This position can also be easily secured as a sequence to a waist lock from behind, should you have been able to trap your opponent into that position while on his feet, or to have risen into it from the ground.

Fig. 8.
HALF-NELSON PARRY AND THROW TO ARM HOLD.

Fig. 9.
A STANDING HALF-NELSON.

A Standing Half-Nelson (Fig. 9).

The half-nelson is of course most frequently employed in ground wrestling, but a standing half-nelson can be sometimes secured at the very commencement of a bout, as shown in Fig. 9. One is not able to exert the same amount of leverage standing as one can when on the ground, but by swinging well round you may bring your man down into a very awkward position (for him), and I can assure you that when a man with such tremendous strength as Mills possesses secures such a grip on you, it is not at all easy to extricate yourself.

Side Arm Lever Hold (Fig. 10).

A good arm throw, which I was fortunate enough to bring off against Relwyskow, is shown in Fig. 10, and may be described as a side arm lever hold. In this I feinted for a buttock, and instead of catching him round the neck, threw my arm through his under the armpit, and so round his waist, at the same time catching his left wrist with my left hand. With my right knee behind him, I was able to easily lever him over on to his back.

A fall which often puts an early termination to a bout is obtained by diving forward while sparring for holds and gripping your opponent round the knees, pulling his legs apart and towards you, throwing the full weight of your shoulders against his hips, and so throwing him on to his back.

A Block to the Leg Grip (Fig. 11).

This hold can be blocked as shown in Fig. 11 in which Relwyskow had dived for my knees, and I

Fig. 10.
SIDE ARM LEVER HOLD.

Fig. 11.
A BLOCK TO THE LEG GRIP.

FIG. 12.
THE CROTCH HOLD.

USEFUL STANDING HOLDS 33

pushed his head down as shown in the illustration. A most simple and effective block, but one in which I was not quite quick enough, for this is really one of his favourite feints for the crotch-hold, the lock to which he is indebted for most of his victories.

THE CROTCH HOLD (Fig. 12).

With a quick twist he freed his head, and sliding his left hand between my legs, slipped his right up to meet it, lifting me off my feet and turning me upside down, to swing me round twice and deposit my shoulders on the mat. Note the position of my hands in Fig. 12, ready to save myself if possible.

WAIST HOLD COUNTER TO KNEE GRAB
(Fig. 13).

The knee grab can be also replied to by the counter which Mills is applying to Beck in Fig. 13. In this he has come forward to Beck's grab, and catching him round the waist from behind, has pulled his feet from the ground. Beck's grab has failed, and Mills has only to swing him slightly outwards to slide him down on to his shoulders.

A KNEE GRIP COUNTER TO WAIST HOLD
(Fig. 14).

A good variety of knee grab is shown in Fig. 14, in which Relwyskow had been caught by Beck in a not too close body-hold in front, and had turned in quickly before the latter could pull him in. He had then stooped down smartly and caught Beck's left knee with both his hands, pulling his foot up

FIG. 13.
WAIST HOLD COUNTER TO KNEE GRAB.

FIG. 14.
A KNEE GRIP COUNTER TO WAIST HOLD.

Fig. 15.
THE "HALCH" OR HEAD THROW.

USEFUL STANDING HOLDS 37

and simultaneously sweeping his right leg away with his own right, throwing himself backwards on top of his opponent. This is a fairly safe counter move to make either to a front body-hold or to a waist-hold from behind, as if you miss your grab or sweep, you can fairly confidently reckon on getting safely on to your hands and knees. Your opponent may, of course, lift you clear from behind if he is quick enough, but then he is well placed to do that anyway, and you are not making your position any worse by your move.

THE "HALCH" OR HEAD THROW (Fig. 15).

One of the best wrestling snapshots I have ever seen depicts a throw of which Hackenschmidt is very fond. It bears various names, but is, I believe, most popularly known as the "halch." To bring it off all that is necessary is to turn in quickly from any standing position, throw your hand or hands round your opponent's head, and stooping well forward to pull him right over your shoulder, as shown in Fig. 15. A fair amount of strength is required, but a well-calculated and timed stoop will make it more a matter of leverage than of strength.

THE DOUBLE BRIDGE (Fig. 16).

Should your opponent "bridge" in defence as he comes down, you can follow up the move by continuing your own bend forward, and "double bridge" on top of him, as in Fig. 16, forcing him gradually down. The weight with which you descend should break his bridge without requiring

Fig. 16.
THE DOUBLE BRIDGE.

Fig. 17.
THE CRADLE HOLD.

Fig. 18.
THE BUTTOCK.

USEFUL STANDING HOLDS 41

any very prolonged pressure, but I must admit that the " double bridge " is a position far more frequently witnessed in exhibition wrestling than in actual contests. It is attractive and effective, but scarcely necessary, as when you have " halched " a man, he ought to go easily enough without any need for further trouble.

The Cradle Hold (Fig. 17).

Another position which is far more frequently seen in display wrestling than in genuine encounters is shown in Fig. 17. In the instance photographed, however, Mills had gone for the crotch-hold as Beck came in for a body-grip, and had grabbed the wrong leg. Beck turned to release himself, and was caught round the neck by Mills' left arm, and then picked up into a cradle-hold and dropped on to his back. The throw can be employed with success as a counter to a forward chancery and bar-hold, provided you are quick enough.

The Buttock and Counter (Figs. 18 and 19).

A good counter to the buttock throw is shown in Fig. 19. I have also included an illustration of the buttock throw itself in operation against Relwyskow in Fig. 18, but Mills, in the illustration shown in the next figure, was too quick. He gripped hands round my waist and lifted me off my feet before I could stoop forward sufficiently far to get him on to my hip, and, in order to save myself against being thrown, I had to counter again by locking in with both legs, thus securing myself against practically any fall.

Fig. 19.
COUNTER TO BUTTOCK AND PARRY.

CHAPTER III

Which deals with Ground Work

A STANDING THROW FOLLOWING A MAT SAFETY DIVE (Fig. 20).

THE position shown in Fig. 20, although depicting a standing throw, was the direct sequence of a ground manœuvre on the part of Sergeant Mills, who, being in an awkward position, went to earth on all fours to avoid being thrown. Beck dived after him, and snatching him round the waist, lifted him bodily. Mills should have grabbed his thighs for safety, but was swung up too quickly. As the reader will observe, he is straining back to avoid being swung outwards and deposited on his shoulders, a fall from which he should not have been allowed to escape.

FURTHER WRIST AND CROTCH HOLD (Fig. 21).

When both have gone to the mat under fairly even conditions, it is often very difficult for either to secure any hold which will prove effective, and supposing both men to be fairly well matched, a fall can frequently be best effected by a surprise move. A trick which I have often found successful is to

FIG. 20.
A STANDING THROW FOLLOWING A SAFETY DIVE TO THE MAT.

Fig. 21.
A FURTHER WAIST AND CROTCH HOLD.

THE LEG HALF-NELSON.

GROUND WORK

play about my opponent's head and shoulders for some little time, and then suddenly diving my left arm say, under him, to grasp his further wrist, and simultaneously securing a crotch-hold with my right, to pull him over on to my knee as shown in Fig. 21. In this position he is pretty helpless, and can without much difficulty be dropped down on to his shoulders.

THE LEG HALF-NELSON (Fig. 22).

The half-nelson is perhaps the hold most generally employed in ground work. I do not think that there is any great need for me to describe this hold, but several of my readers may never have seen the lock illustrated in Fig. 22, which I have called a "leg half-nelson," and which is a hold which the celebrated Bob Somerville was very fond of employing. In the bout from which the photograph was taken I had dived under for a double-leg hold, when Relwyskow turned slightly sideways, and throwing his foot round my neck behind in very similar manner to the ordinary half-nelson position, was able to lever me over with far greater ease, though in an exactly similar fashion to that throw. I would strongly recommend my readers to make a point of studying this manœuvre, as they will often find themselves in positions in which it can be profitably employed.

OFFSIDE OR FURTHER HALF-NELSON (Fig. 23).

That very effective hold, the further offside half-nelson, is excellently illustrated by one which Mills has applied to Beck as shown in Fig. 23. When

Fig. 23.
OFFSIDE, OR FURTHER HALF-NELSON.

FIG. 24.
COUNTER AND RE-COUNTER TO FURTHER HALF-NELSON.

FIG. 25.
COUNTER TO HALF-NELSON.

GROUND WORK

the man securing the hold is resting on his feet, the move can be countered by gripping his ankle, provided that this be near enough to take effective hold of, but possibly the best escape is by " spinning " out.

COUNTER TO FURTHER HALF-NELSON (Fig. 24).

To bridge out of it over your opponent's back is a very risky proceeding, as you are liable to all sorts of fatal locks in transit, and the best method of defending oneself is to counter before the hold is secured. One very usual method is shown to be only partially successful in Fig. 24. Relwyskow here trapped my arm as I was reaching for the hold, and tried an arm roll in imitation of the manner in which Hackenschmidt turned the tables on Madrali. He nearly had me, but just as I was being pulled over his back, I fended myself off by pushing against his head with my left hand, thus creating a deadlock.

COUNTER TO HALF-NELSON (Fig. 25).

A very clever parry to an ordinary half-nelson, which Beck brought off against Mills, is illustrated in Fig. 25. Mills had apparently got well placed when Beck gripped the encircling arm between his arm and side, and rolling over backwards sent the top dog under.

FOLLOWING A HALF-NELSON HOLD (Fig. 26).

In order to ensure the success of a half-nelson hold, it should be assisted, whenever possible, with a crotch, leg or arm hold, and in Fig. 26 Beck is shown lifting Mills' leg in addition to forcing him over

Fig. 26.
CROTCH HOLD IN COMBINATION WITH HALF-NELSON.

Fig. 27.
HALF-NELSON AND FOOT HOLD.

with the half-nelson. He is further pressing this leg into Mills' chest, and can scarcely fail to score a fall.

HALF-NELSON AND FOOT HOLD (Fig. 27).

When a man goes obstinately on to his face and stays there for safety, it is often very difficult to turn him over. In fact it is, as a rule, far more advisable to give up trying and to get up on your feet again, so that the struggle may be commenced afresh. Otherwise, unless you are greatly superior both in science and strength, you will find that you are only wearing yourself out to no purpose. If you can, however, succeed in trapping his foot, as Mills is shown doing in Fig. 27, and can at the same time apply a half-nelson, you should be able to lift and turn him right over on to his shoulders.

HALF-NELSON COUNTER TO GROUND LEG HOLD.
(Fig. 28).

The further half-nelson, employed as a successful counter move in Fig. 28, shows also the danger of reaching underneath for a leg hold when on the ground. In this instance Relwyskow succeeded in trapping my groping arm between his thighs just as I was about to secure a hold, and reaching over to a further half-nelson turned me over on to my shoulders.

GROUND, HEAD AND FURTHER SHOULDER HOLD
(Fig. 29).

A very useful under grip in ground wrestling can be secured by reaching well under your opponent and catching his off shoulder, as I am shown doing in Fig. 29. Simultaneously press his neck down with

FIG. 28.
HALF-NELSON COUNTER TO GROUND LEG HOLD.

Fig. 29.

GROUND, HEAD AND FURTHER SHOULDER HOLD.

FIG. 30.
HALF-NELSON AND LEG HOLD.

your other hand, and he will come over on to his shoulders as easily as possible.

HALF-NELSON AND LEG HOLD (Fig. 30).

In ground wrestling, under grips will be found more easily secured than over grips, and if accompanied by a nelson or ordinary neck or shoulder hold, very little danger of a counter is incurred. Thus a further leg hold in combination with a half-nelson, as shown in Fig. 30, is very effective, and if well secured and the leg pulled in forcibly towards yourself, there is not much chance of your opponent's escaping

A SMASHING FALL (Fig. 31).

The termination of a tremendous bout between Beck and Mills, in which both were " all out," is shown in a somewhat unusual fall, of which Fig. 31 gives a fine representation.

After a lot of finessing Mills got on top, when Beck threw his left arm round his opponent's neck trying for a chancery hold. Mills, in defence, threw himself back, trapping Beck's arm with his head and right hand, at the same time gripping his left leg and thus pulling him clean over on to his shoulders.

AN ESCAPE FROM A FURTHER SHOULDER GRIP (Fig. 32).

In this same bout Mills extricated himself from a very awkward position by " bridging " when in great trouble. Beck had thrown his right arm under, securing his opponent's right shoulder, and at the same time was pulling on his right arm with

Fig. 31.

AN UNUSUAL FALL—COUNTER TO GROUND CHANCERY HOLD.

Fig. 32.
AN ESCAPE FROM A FURTHER SHOULDER GRIP.

GROUND WORK

his own left. Taking a big risk, the sergeant suddenly grabbed out with both hands, throwing his left arm round his antagonist's neck and catching his left shoulder with his right hand, thereby enabling himself to turn over into a bridge for safety. A clever and very daring piece of defensive strategy, which Fig. 32 shows at perhaps its most critical juncture.

ANKLE HOLD COUNTER TO DOUBLE LEG HOLD (Fig. 33).

When an opponent has secured so firm a double-leg hold as that shown in Fig. 33, there would seem to be but small chance of escape from being lifted up and thrown over on to your back. A very quick and clever parry was used, in the form of a dive over the attacker's back and a clutch on his ankle, which pulled him over his head on to his back. Great care had to be exercised to avoid a fatal collision, as the underneath man came over, and although a fall was not secured, an escape was made from a seemingly hopeless position.

COUNTER AND RE-COUNTER TO NECK AND LEG CHANCERY HOLDS (Fig. 34).

Another parry to a very effective neck and leg chancery is shown in Fig. 34. Here we had been kneeling side by side, and my neck had been trapped in a tight chancery. There was only one chance to avoid being downed, and that was to succeed in locking my opponent's left leg between my trapped left leg and my right knee. This I fortunately succeeded in doing, and by throwing my weight

Fig. 33.
ANKLE HOLD COUNTER TO DOUBLE LEG HOLD.

Fig. 34.
COUNTER AND RE-COUNTER TO NECK AND LEG CHANCERY HOLDS.

sideways against my opponent's shoulders to send him over on to his back.

A FAVOURITE HOLD OF MINE (Figs. 35 and 36).

One hold which I always attempt to get in, when struggling on the ground, was snapped in two positions by Mr. Cartwright, and both photographs are, I think, worth reproducing, as they show the commencement and the penultimate stage of the throw. I have heard this hold described as "Ernie's patent," and I must confess that it is one of my especial favourites, as I have never failed to throw any man of anything like my own weight with it once I have managed to secure it on him.

It is by no means a difficult hold to secure, provided it be quickly executed, and can be made to follow on an almost infinite variety of feints. The idea is trap your opponent's head and right shoulder while operating from his left side, and gripping your hands in front of his face, to force his head and shoulder together, feinting to force him over on to his right shoulder, as in Fig. 35. In order to guard against this, he must thrust out his right leg, as a barrier to the leverage exerted, when I suddenly loose my hold, and quickly throwing my right arm under his extended leg, again grip hands and pull him over towards myself, doubling him up as in Fig. 36, so that he has no option but to go down peaceably. I don't know whether it be possible to teach wrestling by written instructions, but this at least is a throw which no one should have any difficulty in practising. I can assure you that it will be found useful.

Fig. 35.
FIRST STAGE OF MY FAVOURITE GROUND THROW.

Fig. 36.
SECOND STAGE.

A Clever Counter to a Double Leg Ground Hold (Fig. 37).

Another patent throw, of which Relwyskow claims to be the inventor, and which he is certainly very fond of employing whenever circumstances permit, is shown in Fig. 37. The necessary position arises when he has apparently laid himself open to a double leg hold when ground wrestling, but has only allowed his opponent to secure a partial grip, so that he will lose his hold when attempting to lift and throw his man. Relwyskow then traps his antagonist's head with his right leg, and, turning, catches hold of his own ankle, pressing his forearm in under the other man's shoulder, and so levering him over on to his back.

Of course in all wrestling contests it is well to bear in mind the ever-present possibility of your adversary lending you his assistance in the compassing of his own defeat. Thus, supposing you wish to turn him to the right, it is advisable to commence by striving to force him to the left, when he, thinking that he has divined your intention, will put out his utmost strength to resist you. As soon as you feel that he is forcing himself round against you, suddenly add your efforts to his and pull him round in the direction in which you originally intended that he should move. If he is as strong or stronger than you are, don't wear yourself out. Let him exert himself, and moving fairly easily, suddenly pull him in the direction in which

Fig. 37.
RELWYSKOW'S "PATENT" COUNTER TO DOUBLE LEG GROUND HOLD.

GROUND WORK

he is pushing you, or push him violently towards the place in which he is pulling you.

Nearly all the ju-jutsu throws are carried out on this principle, and the young wrestler may employ his time far less profitably than in the study of *The Text-book of Ju-jutsu*, by Raku, in which this branch of wrestling is very ably treated. The chapters on Balance and Breakfall also are well worth studying, and pretty nearly every throw dealt with may be profitably employed under catch-as-catch-can rules.

A Ju-Jutsu Throw (Fig. 38).

A striking illustration of the value of apparently yielding to an opponent's attempts to throw you is depicted in Fig. 38, wherein my opponent, having passed his left arm under my left armpit (resting his left hand on my back) and pressing my right shoulder with his right hand, sought to lever me over to the right. I had to go, and preferred that he should go under me, so throwing my imprisoned arm backwards, caught him round the waist behind, threw out my left leg, locking it in his right, and then rolled peacefully over, yielding to his pressure on my back and shoulder, but dragging him down behind and under me. A result which he had scarcely contemplated.

Waist and Neck Ground Hold (Fig. 39).

Another combination of under hold and neck pressure which may be profitably practised is to suddenly slip your right arm underneath and

FIG. 38.
A JU-JUTSU THROW. MAKING MY OPPONENT THROW HIMSELF.

Fig. 39.
WAIST AND NECK GROUND HOLD.

pressing your opponent's head down with your left, to lift him up from the waist downwards, turning him fairly easily on to his shoulders. If this hold be suddenly taken, and you are possessed of sufficient strength, the man will come over all right, as in Fig. 39; but you must turn him quickly to prevent his "spinning out."

Various Under Grips (Fig. 40).

In Fig. 32 was shown a clever escape from an under grip with both arms on an opponent's off shoulder, which foiled an attempt to pull the gripped one over to the right. The best method of applying this throw is to pass the left arm in *front* under the head on to the shoulder, and the right under *behind* the attacked wrestler's right arm, gripping both hands on the shoulder. This can only be resisted, as was shown in Fig. 32, and even then not so effectively, when the attack is made in this manner, or by thrusting out the right leg as a strut, when the hold shown in Figs. 35 and 36 can be brought into play.

Another mode of making this attack is shown in Fig. 40, where I have attacked my opponent's shoulder with my left, passing my hand in front of his chest, and have assisted my pull over by lifting his left leg with my right hand. This throw needs, however, to be very quickly made, and can be resisted by thrusting out the right leg as above, so that considerable strength must be exerted to lever over satisfactorily.

Fig. 40.

AN UNDER GRIP—FURTHER SHOULDER AND LEG HOLD.

Fig. 41.
GROUND HEAD CHANCERY.

FIG. 42.
COUNTER TO STANDING CHANCERY HOLD.

Ground Head Chancery (Fig. 41).

The throw shown in Fig. 41 is one that one often sees employed in wrestling bouts, but is certainly not one to be recommended. It is brought into action when the contestants are head to head, kneeling on the mat, and is a chancery hold with both arms taking a waist-hold and levering over quickly. It is, however, easily countered by trapping the arms round waist with your own arms, and then gathering up the knees, rolling over to either side, when the man on top will go under.

A Counter to a Similar Hold Standing Position (Fig. 42)

A very similar position sometimes arises in stand-up wrestling, which can be similarly countered as shown in Fig. 42. Here the arms, seizing the chancery hold, have been trapped, and the defender is able to hoist his opponent into the air and to throw him overhead. A very nasty fall will result, which can only be avoided by waiting until the grip is loosed preparatory to heaving, and then clutching round neck, or indeed anywhere for safety.

A Selection Of Classic Instructive Titles Relating To
The Art Of Pugilism & Self Defence
In Both War & Peace
Find our entire selection @ naval-military-press.com

ALL-IN FIGHTING
The distilled knowledge of W.E. Fairbairn, legendary SOE instructor in unarmed combat, and inventor of the Sykes-Fairbairn knife, who learned his deadly skills in 30 years on the Shanghai waterfront.
Fully illustrated.
9781847348531

ART OF BOXING AND SCIENCE OF SELF DEFENCE
Former Lightweight Champion Billy Edwards shares the techniques and strategies of the sweet science in his beautifully illustrated boxing guide. Explore boxing's transition from bare knuckle spectacle to today's Marquis of Queensbury ruleset.
9781474539548

SELF DEFENCE OR THE ART OF BOXING
Ned Donnelly was a pioneer of boxing training during the late Victorian era. Explore the strategies and techniques used by this trainer of champions via a series of easy-to-follow illustrations and clear, concise coaching steps.
9781474539562

JACK GOODWIN'S BOXING

This 1920's boxing masterpiece by Jack Goodwin puts you in the shoes of a coach in that era. Uncover the best ways to run, manage and train boxers as taught by Jack Goodwin, a champion and trainer of champions in the noble science.

9781474539586

ART OF WRESTLING

George de Relwyskow Army Gymnastic Staff

In the appreciation to this book Captain Daniels, V.C., M.C., Rifle Brigade, states: "In adding a word to this book on the style of wrestling as taught at the Headquarters Gymnasium of the British Army, and having had personal experience in the various holds and throws taught, I consider it has been of great value in the training of the soldier, and the bringing out of those qualities of grit and determination which have been seen in all ranks who have taken an active part throughout the greatest war in history." 1919.

9781783313563

THE COMPLETE BOXER

Gunner Moir provides detailed instructions on the techniques he deployed to become British Heavyweight Champion. Taught in a series of easy to learn techniques, combinations, and boxing strategies.

9781474539609

BOXING (V-Five)
The Aviation Training Office of the Chief of Naval Operations
The game-changing V-Five suite of training manuals helped get a generation of American aviators fit for war. Here we explore how the airmen of the US navy trained in boxing as part of their military fitness regime.
9781474539623

WRESTLING (V-Five)
The Aviation Training Office of the Chief of Naval Operations
The game-changing V-Five suite of training manuals helped get a generation of American aviators fit for war. Here we explore how the airmen of the US navy trained in collegiate wrestling as part of their military fitness regime.
9781474539685

KILL OR GET KILLED
Rex Applegate's "kill or be killed" helped prepare America's marines, soldiers, sailors, spies and airmen for the realities of war. This highly shared and respected work provides all you need to know about unarmed combat and close quarter engagement with the enemy.
9781474539661

MANUAL OF PHYSICAL TRAINING 1914
(United States Army)
Published just prior to the outbreak of World War 1, this beautifully illustrated guide was designed to revolutionise the combat fitness and readiness of the US Army covering a wide range of gymnastic and combat calisthenic exercises.

DEAL THE FIRST DEADLY BLOW
United States Department of the Army

This Vietnam-era classic showcases in detail how the US Forces trained in close quarter combat. Known as the "encyclopaedia of combat" it helped a generation learn how to become devastating effective with empty hands, knives and bayonets alike.

9781474539722

HAND-TO-HAND COMBAT
Bureau of Aeronautics U.S Navy 1943

This is one of the best combative manuals from World War 2, developed by the US Navy V-Five Staff, that included the renowned American wrestler Wesley Brown. It is then not especially surprising that wrestling skills predominate in this manual, and form the base skill-set for this combative system.

9781474537391

ABWEHR ENGLISCHER GANGSTER METHODEN DEFENSE OF ENGLISH GANGSTERS METHODS – SILENT KILLING – FULL ENGLISH TRANSLATION

In 1942 the Wehrmacht published a training manual with the goal of countering the "silent killing" tactics used by the British commando units. The manual was – much in line with typical National Socialist terminology –titled

"Abwehr Englischer Gangster-methoden" or "Defence Against English Gangster methods".

This book was compiled due the Wehrmacht intelligence operatives uncovering of a British hand-to-hand course for the SOE, Commandos, et al, on methods of quick and silent killing (undoubtedly developed by W. E. Fairbairn and E. A. Sykes). They correctly assessed that their troops in general and particularly the Geheime Staatspolizei (Gestapo), Sicherheitsdienst (SD), their security guards, and sentries would be in grave danger when confronted by men trained in these methods. This manual/program was the Wehrmacht's response.

9781474538336

HAND TO HAND COMBAT

Francois d'Eliscu taught thousands of U.S. Army Rangers how to fight down and dirty in World War II. d'Eliscu doesn't get the press that Fairbairn and Applegate do, but he did a commendable job writing this book. It is basic, meant for training raw recruits in a short amount of time before sending them to the front, but simple is good when you are in combat, as most combative experts' will tell you.

9781474535823

WE Fairbairn's Complete Compendium of Lethal, Unarmed, Hand-to-Hand Combat Methods and Fighting In Colour

All 844 images of Fairbairn and his assistants can now for the first time be seen in full colour, lending a clarity to the practical methods of mastering the manner of dealing with an assailant, both in time of war and when placed in difficulty during unpleasant modern urban situations. These various holds, trips, kicks, blows etc, allow the average man or woman a position of security against almost any form of armed or unarmed attack.

Captain W.E. Fairbairn would have approved of this new colour version, that gives an illustrative clarity to the original that was lacking in previous monochrome reprints of his work.

All six of W.E. Fairbairn's works in one binding to create the ultimate colour compendium: Get Tough-All-In Fighting-Shooting to Live-Scientific Self-Defence-Hands Off!-Defendu

9781783318735

BOXING FOR BOYS

Regtl. Sergt.-Major & B Dent Army Gymnastic Headquarters

A successful system of boxing instruction for large classes, to allow tuition with no detriment to the "backward or shy pupil". Covers Kit-On, Guard-Sparring-Advance-Point & Mark-Ducking-Medicine, Bag-Left & Right Hooks etc. The author considered that boxing systematically taught to the youth was beneficial exercise, and would have a marked elevating influence on the national character.

9781783314607

HAND-TO-HAND FIGHTING

A System Of Personal Defence For The Soldier (1918)

A tough book on the art of hand to hand fighting in the trenches of the Great War. Demonstrating techniques utilised to "do away with the enemy", many of which are barred in clean wrestling, the book includes good clear photographic illustrations presenting important attack methods including the "Hammer Lock", "Kidney Kick", "Head Twist", "Knee Groin Kick", and the "Knee Break", all very important in a man to man, life or death encounter, when fighting in the mud of the trenches.

9781783313983

www.ingramcontent.com/pod-product-compliance
Lightning Source LLC
Chambersburg PA
CBHW071316110426
42743CB00042B/2583